FRETBOARD FORENSICS SERIES ™

FOR GUITAR

POSITION X AND THE TWELVE SHAPE THEOREM

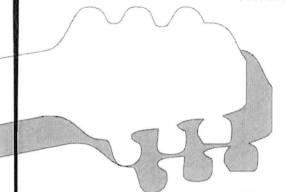

by

Walter Klosowski III

is published exclusively through:

OMNI MUSIC PRESS ®

http://www.omnimusicpress.com

Written, designed, edited, compiled, printed & distributed by the author.

Order Number OMP 002-001

FOR GUITAR

AND THE TWELVE SHAPE THEOREM

Walter Klosowski III

OMP®

OMNI MUSIC PRESS

Table of Contents

Preface   i

The ①ˢᵗ / ⑥ᵗʰ String(s), 2ⁿᵈ Finger Shapes   01
..."The G Flat / F Sharp Shapes"

The ①ˢᵗ / ⑥ᵗʰ String(s), 3ʳᵈ Finger Shapes   07
..."The G Shapes"

The ①ˢᵗ / ③ʳᵈ / ⑥ᵗʰ String(s), 1ˢᵗ & 4ᵗʰ Finger Shapes   13
..."The A Flat / G Sharp Shapes"

The ③ʳᵈ String, 2ⁿᵈ Finger Shapes   19
..."The A Shapes"

The ③ʳᵈ String, 3ʳᵈ Finger Shapes   25
..."The B Flat / A Sharp Shapes"

The ⑤ᵗʰ String, 2ⁿᵈ Finger Shapes   31
..."The B Shapes"

The ⑤ᵀᴴ String, 3ᴿᴰ Finger Shapes   37
..."The C Shapes"

The ②ᴺᴰ String, 2ᴺᴰ Finger Shapes   43
..."The D Flat / C Sharp Shapes"

The ②ᴺᴰ String, 3ᴿᴰ Finger Shapes   49
..."The D Shapes"

The ②ᴺᴰ / ④ᵀᴴ String(s), 1ˢᵀ & 4ᵀᴴ Finger Shapes   55
..."The E Flat / D Sharp Shapes"

The ④ᵀᴴ String, 2ᴺᴰ Finger Shapes   61
..."The E Shapes"

The ④ᵀᴴ String, 3ᴿᴰ Finger Shapes   67
..."The F Shapes"

APPENDIX   73

This book is dedicated to all those who love guitar and pursue its study. As for writing it, I owe a deep personal thank you to my family, all of whom supported me and gave of their time during this project. I would also like to thank my music professors, colleagues, students and friends for answering my questions concerning this material and sharing their own answers, opinions and insights.

POSITION X AND THE TWELVE SHAPE THEOREM ...

... IS A DIFFERENT KIND OF GUITAR CHORD AND SCALE BOOK IN THAT HERE, ALL THE SHAPES ARE MOVABLE TO, AND AT THE SAME TIME FIT IN, ANY SINGLE POSITION. POSITION X ASSUMES THE FOLLOWING:

1) GUITAR POSITION DETAIL

SIX IS THE EXACT NUMBER OF CONSECUTIVE FRETS INVOLVED IN A GUITAR POSITION AND EACH POSITION SPANS TWO OCTAVES PLUS A PERFECT FOURTH...

2) THE FRETTING HAND

THE 2ND & 3RD FINGERS REMAIN STATIONARY, ALLOWING THE OTHER FINGERS TO STRETCH JUST A FRET...

3) THE PICKING HAND

A ①, ③, ⑤, ②, ④, ⑥ PICKING PATTERN OCCURS UNDER THE 2ND & 3RD FINGERS WHEN THE NOTES ARE PLACED IN CHROMATIC OR ALPHABETICAL ORDER...

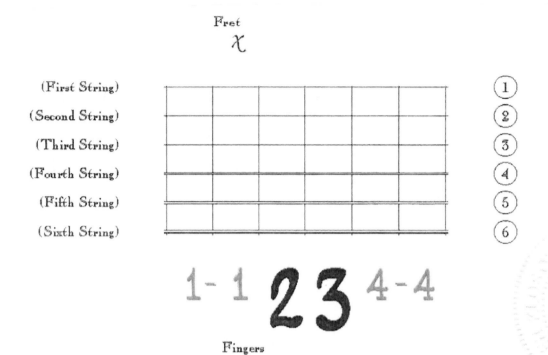

Fret
X

(First String) — 1
(Second String) — 2
(Third String) — 3
(Fourth String) — 4
(Fifth String) — 5
(Sixth String) — 6

1- 1 **2 3** 4 -4

Fingers

This grid represents the guitar position as used in this book. The thinnest string is on top and it has six consecutive frets. The four fingered fretting hand centers itself inside the six frets, one finger per fret, with an additional fret on each side. The fret immediately behind the 2ND finger determines position location. This initial consecutive four fret area makes for a complete chromatic universe all unto itself. In fact, a great deal of position work can be traced back to the initial four frets. When expanding to the total six, it is critical to realize that the 2ND & 3RD fingers remain stationary where

THEY ARE. THEY DO NOT STRETCH AND THERE IS NEVER A FRET BETWEEN THEM. THE 2ND & 3RD FINGERS REMAIN POISED LIKE THEY DO, AT THE READY, BECAUSE THE STATIONARY QUALITIES ALLOW THE FIRST FINGER AND FOURTH FINGER TO STRETCH THAT ADDITIONAL FRET WHEN NEEDED. LOOK AT THE POSITION FINGERING DETAILED IN THE EXAMPLE BELOW FOR ANY CLARIFICATION.

POSITION X FINGERING DETAIL COMPLETE WITH STRETCHES

X

1- 1 2 3 4 -4

⌒ POSITION NUMBER BEHIND SECOND FINGER, ONE FINGER PER FRET

THE X IMPLIES THE "RANDOM POSITION", WHICH AGAIN IS DETERMINED BY THE FRET BEHIND THE 2ND FINGER SINCE THE FIRST FINGER MAY STRETCH. THAT OCCASIONAL FIRST FINGER STRETCH, COUPLED WITH THE OCCASIONAL FOURTH FINGER STRETCH, ROUNDS OUT THE SIX CONSECUTIVE FRET AREA AS DISCUSSED. ANY CONSECUTIVE SIX FRETS ON THE GUITAR FRETBOARD WILL SPAN A MUSICAL TWO OCTAVES PLUS A PERFECT FOURTH, AS LONG AS THE GUITAR REMAINS IN STANDARD TUNING. AND, OF COURSE, EVERYTHING REPEATS ONCE PAST THE TWELFTH FRET.

THESE ARE THE FOUR CHORD TYPES AS PRESENTED IN THIS BOOK. BOTH ROWS PROVIDE ALTERNATE MATERIAL CHOICE.

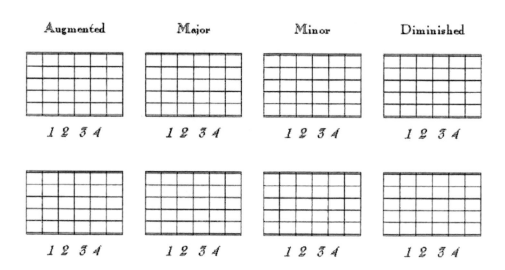

THE ORDER OR SEQUENCE OF THE CHORDS AS PRESENTED IN THIS TEXT IS PURPOSEFUL AND IMPORTANT. AS THE EYES MOVE ACROSS THE PAGE FROM LEFT TO RIGHT, OR RIGHT TO LEFT, ONLY ONE NOTE OR PITCH CHANGES. FOR EXAMPLE, AS THE AUGMENTED CHORD MOVES TO THE MAJOR, ONLY THE FIFTH WILL CHANGE. AS THE MAJOR MOVES TO THE MINOR, ONLY THE THIRD WILL CHANGE. AS THE MINOR MOVES TO THE DIMINISHED, ONLY THE FIFTH WILL CHANGE. TWO NOTES ALWAYS STAYING THE SAME WITH ONE NOTE CHANGING IS VERY EFFECTIVE. THE TOP GRID ROW DETAILS THE GIVEN CHORD TYPES. ANY MATERIAL ASSOCIATED WITH THE SPECIFIC CHORD TYPE IS THEN PLACED UNDERNEATH.

Augmented Chord – (Brings Musical Tension)

This chord type consists of a major third interval placed on top of another major third interval. From the root note it's a major third with an augmented fifth.

Major Chord – (Brings Musical Stability)

This chord type consists of a major third interval placed on top of a minor third interval. From the root note it's a major third as well, but this time with a perfect fifth.

Minor Chord – (Brings Musical Stability)

This chord type consists of a minor third interval placed on top of a major third interval. From the root note it's a minor third interval and a perfect fifth.

Diminished Chord – (Brings Musical Tension)

This chord type consists of a minor third placed on top of another minor third. From the root note it's a minor third interval now with a diminished fifth.

These are the four scale types as presented in this book. Both rows provide alternate material choice.

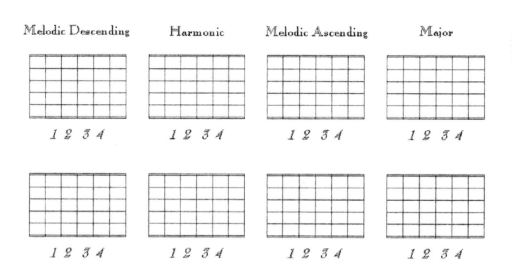

Melodic Descending   Harmonic   Melodic Ascending   Major

1 2 3 4   1 2 3 4   1 2 3 4   1 2 3 4

1 2 3 4   1 2 3 4   1 2 3 4   1 2 3 4

As the eyes move across the page left to right, or right to left, only one note or pitch changes. When the melodic minor descending form moves to the harmonic minor form, only the seventh scale degree changes. As the harmonic minor form moves to the melodic minor ascending form, only the sixth scale degree changes. The melodic minor ascending form to the major scale?...only the third changes. The perspective of everything staying in place with one note changing is the very effective. Both grid rows detail the given scales and other material associated with them or the given shape in this book.

Melodic minor scale descending form

This scale type is the same as the aeolian, natural or pure minor, and the pentatonic is derived from it as well. The given "three on a string" pentatonic is placed under the given melodic minor in this book.

Harmonic minor scale

This scale type represents the traditional minor scale as taught in the various music textbooks, reference and methods. It is presented as that opposite to the blissful sounding major scale.

Melodic minor scale ascending form

This scale type is also known as the jazz minor. It traditionally complements the descending melodic minor form just the same.

Major scale

This scale type is most important as a great deal of other musical material is based on it, specifically the minor keys and modes. The major scale is also used to demonstrate other musical concepts.

THE ①ST / ⑥TH STRING(S), 2ND FINGER SHAPES

..."THE G FLAT / F SHARP SHAPES"

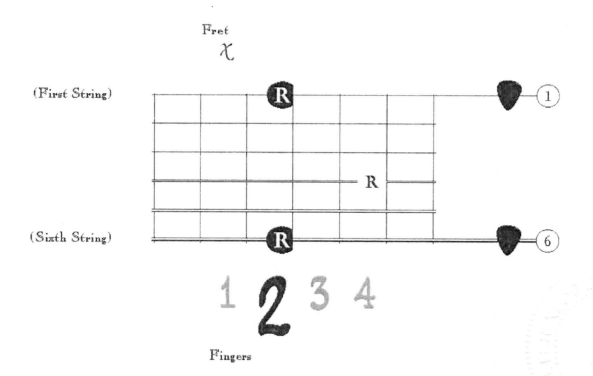

Fret
𝒳

(First String)

R

R

(Sixth String)

R

1

6

1 2 3 4

Fingers

THIS IS THE FIRST / SIXTH STRING(S), SECOND FINGER SHAPE. ITS MAIN ROOT NOTE(S) ARE FOUND ON THE FIRST / SIXTH STRING(S) UNDER THE SECOND FINGER AND THE SECOND FINGER USUALLY PLAYS THEM. THE ONLY OTHER ROOT NOTE HERE IS USUALLY PLAYED WITH THE FOURTH FINGER. FUNCTIONAL TENSION DICTATES THAT THE SECOND AND FOURTH FINGERS OF THE FRETTING HAND WORK IN TANDEM WHEN PLAYING THIS PROPRIETARY CHORD AND SCALE MATERIAL. ⇨

SOME OF THE GUITAR CHORD SHAPES ASSOCIATED WITH THIS **MAIN** ROOT NOTE(S) ARE:

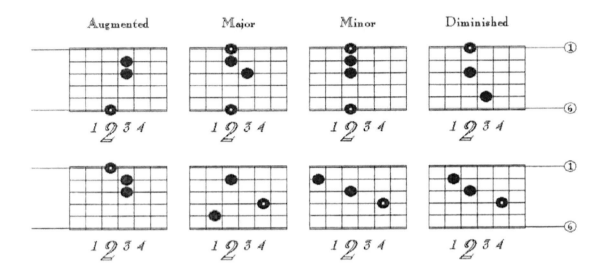

SOME OF THE GUITAR SCALE SHAPES ASSOCIATED WITH THIS **MAIN** ROOT NOTE(S) ARE:

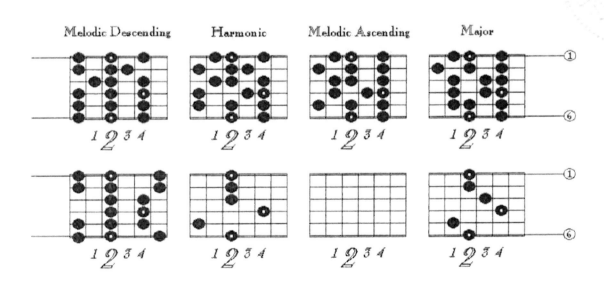

Further Commentary...

All first / sixth string(s) second finger shapes, as listed on the previous page, are entirely movable and fit neatly into any single position along the guitar fretboard.

It is extremely important to notice that there are two MAIN root note(s) present under the second finger here. Consequently, the second finger on the fretting hand may voice the MAIN root note(s) separately, using the thinnest or thickest string, or it can barre them together in some chord voicing that involves all six strings. Either way, as the fingering process unfolds, the second finger on the fretting hand maintains a sort of natural distinction over the other fingers

SIMPLY BECAUSE BOTH **MAIN** ROOT NOTE(S) FALL UNDERNEATH IT AND IT ALONE.

IN CLOSING, THERE IS JUST ONE OTHER ROOT NOTE ASSOCIATED WITH THESE TWO **MAIN** ROOT NOTE(S) LEFT TO DISCUSS, AND IT IS LOCATED ON THE FOURTH STRING. PLEASE USE THE FOURTH FINGER TO PLAY IT. THE GIVEN CHORD AND SCALE MATERIAL FOUND ON THE PREVIOUS PAGE CLEARLY SHOWS THAT THIS ROOT NOTE IS OFTEN PAIRED WITH EITHER OF THE TWO **MAIN** ROOT NOTE(S) IN QUESTION.

ALL THE ROOT NOTES SIMPLY FUNCTION AS FOCAL POINTS IN THIS MATERIAL. BUT NOT EVERY ROOT NOTE NEEDS TO BE VOICED SIMULTANEOUSLY.

THE
①ST / ⑥TH STRING(S),
3RD FINGER SHAPES

..."THE G SHAPES"

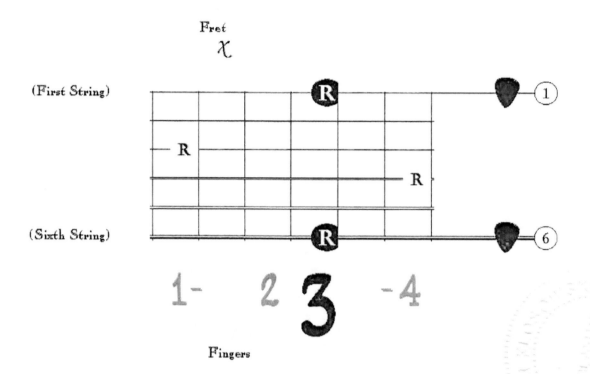

Fret
X

(First String)

R

R

R

R

1

(Sixth String)

R

6

1- 2 **3** -4

Fingers

THIS IS THE FIRST / SIXTH STRING(S), THIRD
FINGER SHAPE. ITS **MAIN** ROOT NOTE(S) ARE
FOUND ON THE FIRST / SIXTH STRING(S) UNDER
THE THIRD FINGER AND THE THIRD FINGER USUALLY
PLAYS THEM. THE OTHER ROOT NOTES ARE FOUND
ON THE RESPECTIVE THIRD AND FOURTH STRINGS
AND REQUIRE FINGER STRETCHES TO PLAY. THE
THIRD FINGER AND STRETCHED FIRST FINGER OF
THE FRETTING HAND WORK IN TANDEM WHEN
PLAYING THROUGH THIS PROPRIETARY MATERIAL. ⇨

SOME OF THE GUITAR CHORD SHAPES ASSOCIATED WITH THIS MAIN ROOT NOTE(S) ARE:

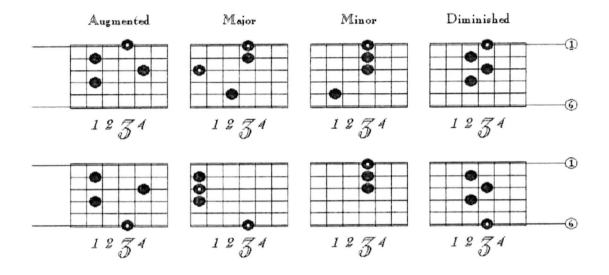

SOME OF THE GUITAR SCALE SHAPES ASSOCIATED WITH THIS MAIN ROOT NOTE(S) ARE:

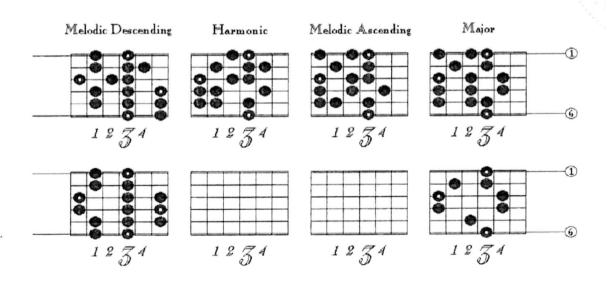

FURTHER COMMENTARY...

ALL THE FIRST / SIXTH STRING(S) THIRD FINGER SHAPES ON THE PREVIOUS PAGE ARE ENTIRELY MOVABLE AND FIT NEATLY INTO ANY POSITION ALONG THE GUITAR FRETBOARD.

WHEN VOICING THEM, THE THIRD FINGER OF THE FRETTING HAND MAY OPT TO VOICE THE INDIVIDUAL **MAIN** ROOT NOTE(S) SEPARATELY OR IT CAN BUDDY UP WITH THE FOURTH FINGER TO PLAY BOTH **MAIN** ROOT NOTE(S) SIMULTANEOUSLY. EITHER WAY, THE THIRD FINGER MAINTAINS A SORT OF PRECEDENCE DURING THE FINGERING PROCESS AS BOTH **MAIN** ROOT NOTES FALL UNDERNEATH IT.

THE ROOT NOTE FOUND ON THE THIRD STRING IS OFTEN PAIRED WITH EITHER OF THESE **MAIN** ROOT

NOTE(S) IN THE GIVEN SHAPE MATERIAL. IT
REQUIRES A FIRST FINGER STRETCH TO PLAY.

IN CLOSING, THE ONLY OTHER ROOT NOTE THAT
REMAINS IS OF THE SAME PITCH AS THE LATTER
BUT FOUND ON THE ADJACENT FOURTH STRING. IT
REQUIRES A FOURTH FINGER STRETCH TO PLAY,
TECHNICALLY SPEAKING, BUT MOST JUST SLIDE
INTO IT AND FROM IT WITH THE FOURTH FINGER.

ALL ROOT NOTES ARE SIMPLY MEANT TO FUNCTION
AS MUSICAL FOCAL POINTS IN THE MATERIAL. BUT
NOT EVERY ROOT NOTE HAS TO BE PRESENT, NOR
PRESENT SIMULTANEOUSLY, WHEN VOICING ANY
CHORD OR SCALE.

The
①ˢᵗ / ③ᴿᴰ / ⑥ᵀᴴ String(s),
1ˢᵗ & 4ᵀᴴ Finger Shapes

..."The A Flat / G Sharp Shapes"

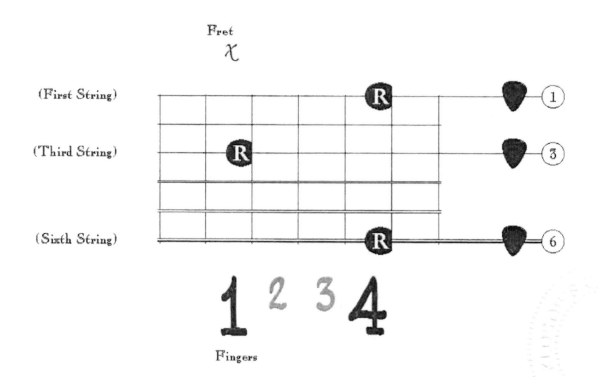

THIS IS THE FIRST / THIRD / SIXTH STRING(S), FIRST AND FOURTH FINGER SHAPE. THE NAME COMES FROM THE **MAIN** ROOT NOTE(S) BEING FOUND ON THE FIRST / THIRD / SIXTH STRING(S) UNDER THE FIRST AND FOURTH FINGERS. INCIDENTALLY, THE FIRST AND FOURTH FINGERS PLAY THEM MOST OF THE TIME. NOTICE THIS SHAPE HAS NO OTHER ROOT NOTES IN IT BEYOND THE **MAIN** ROOT NOTE(S), AND AS SUCH, THE FIRST AND FOURTH FINGERS OF THE FRETTING HAND WORK BEST WHEN PLAYING THIS MATERIAL. ⇨

SOME OF THE GUITAR CHORD SHAPES ASSOCIATED WITH THIS <u>MAIN</u> ROOT NOTE(S) ARE:

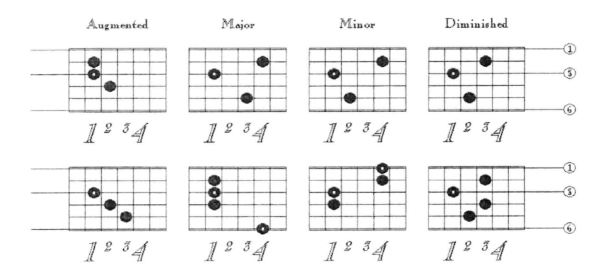

SOME OF THE GUITAR SCALE SHAPES ASSOCIATED WITH THIS <u>MAIN</u> ROOT NOTE(S) ARE:

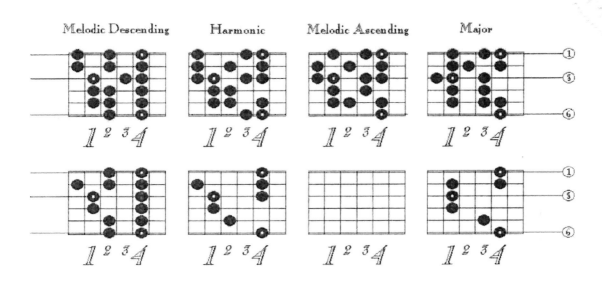

FURTHER COMMENTARY...

ALL FIRST / THIRD / SIXTH STRING(S) FIRST AND
FOURTH FINGER SHAPES FOUND ON THE PREVIOUS
PAGE FIT NICELY INTO ANY GUITAR POSITION. ALL
ARE MOVABLE TO ANY OTHER AS WELL.

THIS SHAPE IS UNIQUE IN THAT THERE ARE THREE
MAIN ROOT NOTES PRESENT IN IT. CONSEQUENTLY,
THE FIRST AND FOURTH FINGERS OF THE FRETTING
HAND MAY OPT TO VOICE THEM INDIVIDUALLY, LIKE IN
AN ARPEGGIO OR SCALE. OR IT MAY DO THE SAME
USING ONE OR TWO IN A CHORD. BUT NO MATTER
WHAT THE VOICING MAY INCLUDE, IT IS FUNCTIONAL
TENSION THAT DICTATES THE FIRST AND FOURTH
FINGERS MAINTAIN A DISTINCT PRECEDENCE IN THE
FINGERING SITUATION AS ALL THE **MAIN** ROOT NOTE(S)
FALL UNDERNEATH THEM.

ALL **MAIN** ROOT NOTE(S) DO IS ACT AS MUSICAL
FOCAL POINTS WITHIN THE GIVEN CHORD AND SCALE
MATERIAL. BUT NOT ALL THREE **MAIN** ROOT NOTE(S)
NEED BE PRESENT, NOR PRESENT SIMULTANEOUSLY,
WHEN IT COMES TO VOICING ANY CHORD OR SCALE.

THE
③RD STRING,
2ND FINGER SHAPES

..."THE A SHAPES"

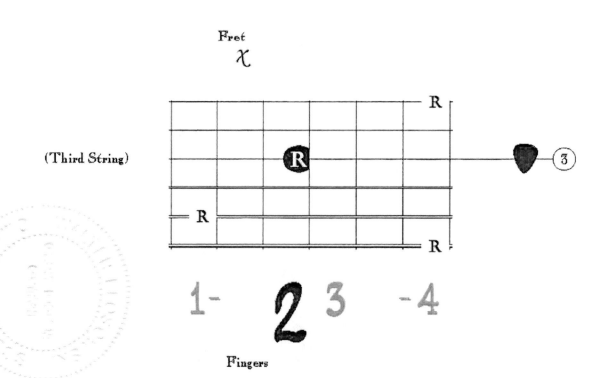

Fret

X

(Third String)

Fingers

1- **2** 3 -4

THIS IS THE THIRD STRING SECOND FINGER SHAPE.
IT GETS ITS NAME FROM THE MAIN ROOT NOTE BEING
FOUND ON THE THIRD STRING UNDER THE SECOND
FINGER. THE SECOND FINGER PLAYS IT NEARLY ALL
THE TIME. THE OTHER ROOT NOTES ARE FOUND ON
THE FIRST, FIFTH AND SIXTH STRINGS RESPECTFULLY,
EACH REQUIRING A FINGER STRETCH TO PLAY. HERE,
FUNCTIONAL TENSION DICTATES THAT THE SECOND
AND FOURTH FINGERS WORK TOGETHER WHEN VOICING
THIS MATERIAL. ⇨

SOME OF THE GUITAR CHORD SHAPES ASSOCIATED WITH THIS MAIN ROOT NOTE ARE:

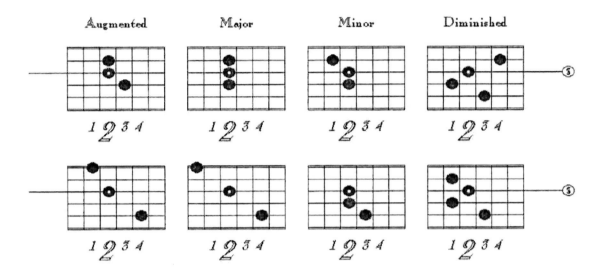

SOME OF THE GUITAR SCALE SHAPES ASSOCIATED WITH THIS MAIN ROOT NOTE ARE:

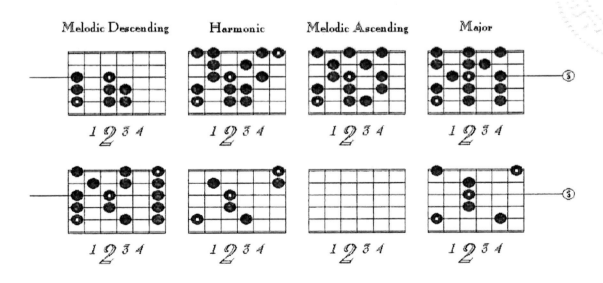

Further Commentary...

All third string second finger shapes listed on the previous page fit neatly into any single guitar position. Previously mastered in the one, they can then spread to any other; all material being movable. In doing so it is a good idea to experiment with the open strings.

When voicing the material here remember to keep the second finger stationary. This is especially important when voicing a chord or scale that uses a finger stretch. Also, it is quite common for the second finger to barre a neighboring string and it is also quite common for the second finger to buddy with another finger, in the same fret, to help voice a chord or scale.

NOTICE THE LOWER OCTAVE ROOT NOTE FOUND ON THE FIFTH STRING IS OFTEN USED WITH THIS **MAIN** ROOT NOTE. THE STRETCHED FIRST FINGER PLAYS IT. INCIDENTALLY, THE STRETCHED FIRST FINGER ALSO HAS A NATURAL INCLINATION TO FRET THE THINNEST STRING WHEN CHORDING. THE REMAINING ROOT NOTES ARE PLAYED WITH THE STRETCHED FOURTH FINGER, STRETCHING TO THE ROOT NOTE(S) FOUND ON THE FIRST / SIXTH STRING(S). HOWEVER, MOST JUST SLIDE TO AND FROM THE GIVEN ROOT NOTE RATHER THAN STRETCH.

ALL ROOT NOTES ACT AS MUSICAL POINTS WITHIN THE GIVEN MATERIAL. BUT NOT EVERY ROOT NOTE NEEDS TO BE PRESENT WHEN VOICING ANY CHORD OR SCALE.

THE
③ᴿᴰ STRING,
3ᴿᴰ FINGER SHAPES

...ˮThe B Flat / A Sharp Shapesˮ

Fret

X

(Third String)

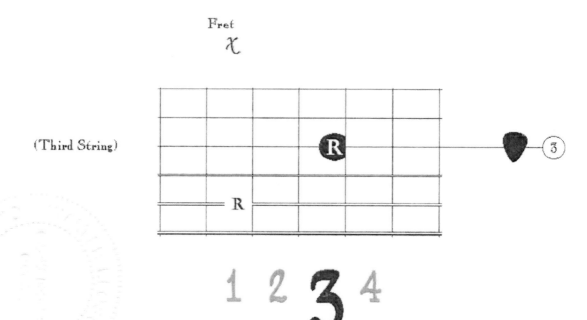

Fingers

THIS IS THE THIRD STRING THIRD FINGER SHAPE. ITS
MAIN ROOT NOTE IS FOUND ON THE THIRD STRING
UNDER THE THIRD FINGER, HENCE THE TITLE. THE
THIRD FINGER PLAYS IT NEARLY ALL THE TIME. THE
OTHER ROOT NOTE, LOCATED AN OCTAVE BELOW ON
THE FIFTH STRING, IS OFTEN PAIRED WITH THIS **MAIN**
ROOT NOTE. USE THE FIRST FINGER TO PLAY IT, NO
STRETCH NEEDED. THE THIRD AND FIRST FINGERS OF
THE FRETTING HAND WORK IN TANDEM WHEN PLAYING
THIS MATERIAL. ⇨

SOME OF THE GUITAR CHORD SHAPES ASSOCIATED WITH THIS MAIN ROOT NOTE ARE:

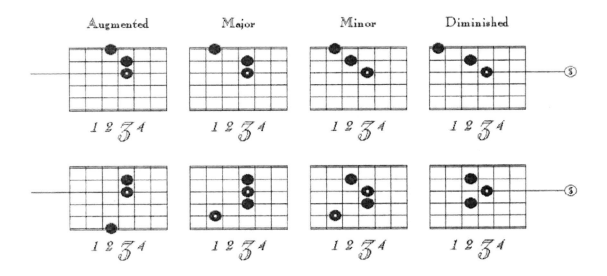

SOME OF THE GUITAR SCALE SHAPES ASSOCIATED WITH THIS MAIN ROOT NOTE ARE:

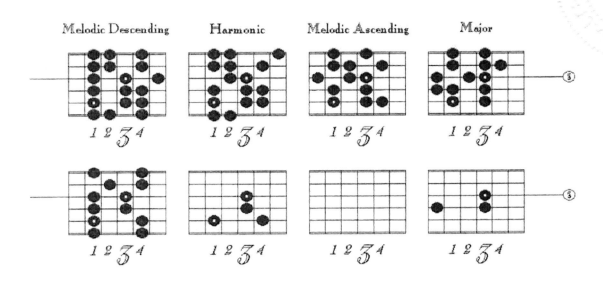

Further commentary...

All third string third finger chord and scale shapes work well in any guitar position. It works best to pick out one position first and learn the shapes there before moving them freely about the neck of the guitar.

When voicing this material it is best that the third finger remain stationary, hovering over the strings in the specified fret area. This is because the third finger is involved all the time in fretting the strings there, whether it be a fancy chord or simple scale. The third finger can barre any number of strings too or it can buddy with the fourth finger to help maintain the overall third finger situation. So, for the sake of functional tension, it is best

THAT THE THIRD FINGER HOVERS OVER THE SPECIFIED FRET AREA WHERE THE **MAIN** ROOT NOTE IS, READY TO PLAY, POISED IN ACTION.

ALSO FACTOR IN THE OBSCURED POWER FIVE CHORD WITHIN THE SHAPES HERE. NOT ALWAYS, BUT OFTEN ENOUGH, THE POPULAR POWER FIVE IS PLACED ON THE THICKER STRINGS AND YES GUITARISTS READILY TAKE ADVANTAGE OF ITS PRACTICALITY ALL TOO OFTEN BY MOVING IT UP AND DOWN THE NECK. THE MATERIAL DISPLAYED HERE DOES INCLUDE THE SAME POWER FIVE CHORD STRUCTURE, EMBEDDED ON THE FIFTH STRING THAT IS, BUT REMEMBER THE THIRD FINGER HAS THE **MAIN** ROOT NOTE AND NOT THE FIRST. AND, AS ALWAYS, NOT EVERY ROOT NOTE NEED BE VOICED ALL THE TIME.

THE
⑤TH STRING,
2ND FINGER SHAPES

..."THE 8 SHAPES"

Fret
χ

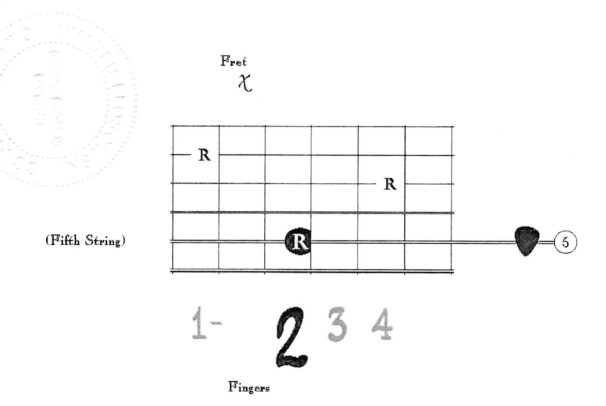

(Fifth String)

1- **2** 3 4

Fingers

THIS IS THE FIFTH STRING SECOND FINGER SHAPE.
THE NAME COMES FROM THE **MAIN** ROOT NOTE BEING
FOUND ON THE FIFTH STRING, UNDER THE SECOND
FINGER. THE SECOND FINGER SEEMS TO PLAY IT ALL
THE TIME. THE OTHER ROOT NOTES ARE FOUND ON
THE SECOND AND THIRD STRINGS, ONE OCTAVE
HIGHER. THE STRETCHED FIRST FINGER PLAYS THE
FORMER AND FOURTH FINGER PLAYS THE LATTER.
HERE, FUNCTIONAL TENSION SHOWS WHY THE SECOND
AND FOURTH FINGERS WORK BEST TOGETHER. ⇨

SOME OF THE GUITAR CHORD SHAPES ASSOCIATED WITH THIS MAIN ROOT NOTE ARE:

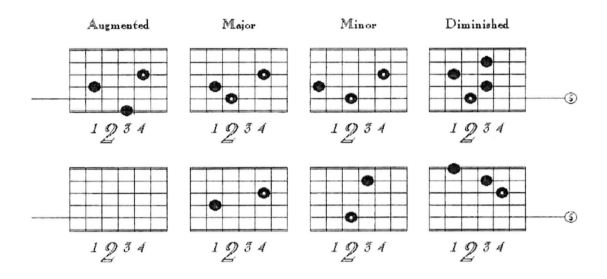

SOME OF THE GUITAR SCALE SHAPES ASSOCIATED WITH THIS MAIN ROOT NOTE ARE:

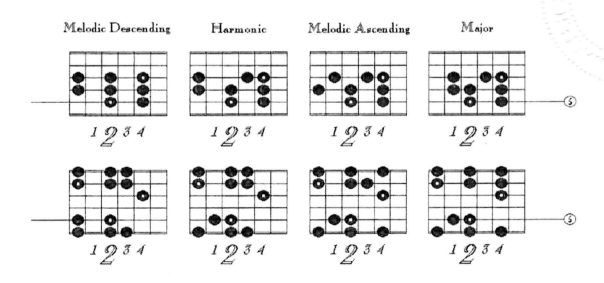

FURTHER COMMENTARY...

ALL FIFTH STRING SECOND FINGER SHAPES LISTED ON THE PREVIOUS PAGE FIT NEATLY INTO ANY SINGLE GUITAR POSITION AND ALL CAN BE MOVED TO ANY OTHER AS WELL. PICK A POSITION AND LEARN THE SHAPES THERE FIRST PRIOR TO MOVING THEM UP AND DOWN THE NECK.

IDEALLY, WHEN PLAYING THESE SHAPES, THE SECOND FINGER SHOULD HOVER JUST ABOVE THE FRET WHERE THE **MAIN** ROOT NOTE IS. DOING SO MAKES IT EASIER TO ORIENTATE THE MATERIAL AROUND THE SECOND FINGER AND ALLOWS FOR IMPROVED FINGERING. ALSO, AS THE MATERIAL SHOWS, THE HIGHER PITCHED ROOT NOTE FOUND ON THE THIRD STRING OFTEN PAIRS ITSELF WITH THIS **MAIN** ROOT NOTE. BE SURE TO USE THE FOURTH FINGER TO PLAY IT.

THE ONLY OTHER REMAINING ROOT NOTE TO DEAL
WITH IS FOUND ON THE ADJACENT SECOND STRING.
IT IS IN UNISON WITH THE PREVIOUS ROOT NOTE BUT
IT REQUIRES A FIRST FINGER STRETCH TO PLAY. THE
PECULIAR LOCATION OF THIS ROOT NOTE COUPLED
WITH ITS UNISON STATUS LEADS TO SOME UNIQUE
FINGERING OPTIONS FOR VOICING THESE CHORDS AND
SCALES.

ALL ROOT NOTES FOUND IN THESE FIFTH STRING
SECOND FINGER SHAPES MERELY ACT AS SMALL FOCAL
POINTS WITHIN THE GIVEN MATERIAL. BUT IN MUSIC
NOT EVERY ROOT NOTE NEED BE PRESENT, NOR
PRESENT SIMULTANEOUSLY, WHEN IT COMES TO ANY
CHORD OR SCALE VOICING.

THE
⑤TH STRING,
3RD FINGER SHAPES

..."THE C SHAPES"

Fret
X

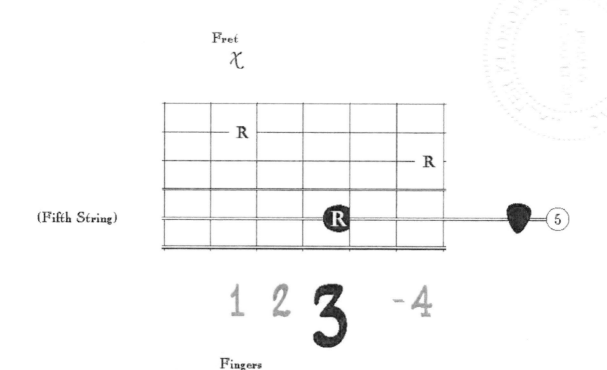

(Fifth String)

1 2 **3** ⁻4

Fingers

THIS IS THE FIFTH STRING THIRD FINGER SHAPE. IT
GETS ITS NAME FROM THE MAIN ROOT NOTE BEING
FOUND ON THE FIFTH STRING UNDER THE THIRD
FINGER. THE THIRD FINGER DOES THE FRETTING.
THE OTHER ROOT NOTES INVOLVED ARE FOUND ON
THE SECOND AND THIRD STRINGS AN OCTAVE AWAY.
USE THE FIRST FINGER TO PLAY THE FORMER AND
THE STRETCHED FOURTH FINGER TO PLAY THE
LATTER. NOTICE HOW THE THIRD AND FIRST FINGERS
OF THE FRETTING HAND WORK IN TANDEM HERE. ⇨

SOME OF THE GUITAR CHORD SHAPES ASSOCIATED WITH THIS **MAIN** ROOT NOTE ARE:

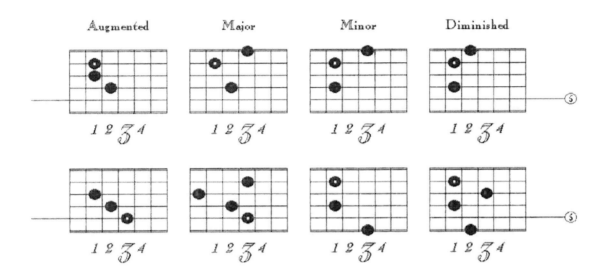

SOME OF THE GUITAR SCALE SHAPES ASSOCIATED WITH THIS **MAIN** ROOT NOTE ARE:

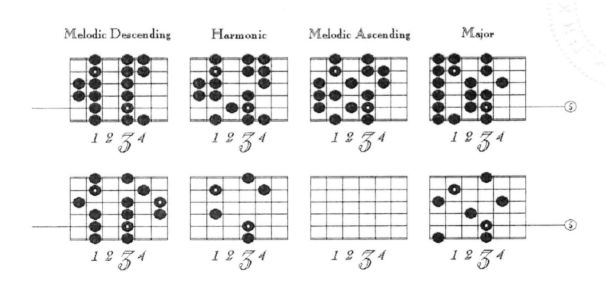

FURTHER COMMENTARY...

ALL FIFTH STRING THIRD FINGER SHAPES FIT NEATLY INTO ANY ONE OF THE MANY AVAILABLE POSITIONS ALONG THE NECK AND ALL SHAPES ARE MOVABLE AS WELL. CHOOSE A POSITION THAT FITS BEST AND LEARN THE MATERIAL THERE BEFORE FREELY MOVING THESE SHAPES ABOUT THE NECK.

WHEN PLAYING THESE SHAPES THE THIRD FINGER ON THE FRETTING HAND IS TO REMAIN STATIONARY, OR AT THE VERY LEAST HOVER ABOVE, THE RESPECTIVE FRET AREA. DOING SO FOSTERS GREAT TECHNIQUE AS THAT'S WHERE THE **MAIN** ROOT NOTE IS FOUND, LIKE A VISUAL ANCHOR IN THE FINGERING SITUATION.

THE OTHER ROOT NOTES, LOCATED AN OCTAVE AWAY, ARE IN UNISON AND FOUND ON A PAIR OF STRINGS.

However, the root note that is located on the second string is very important because it is the one often paired with the **main** root note in question. As the given stock material clearly shows, it is self evident why the first finger plays this root note nearly all the time.

The last root note involved here is found on the third string. It requires a fourth finger stretch to play, technically speaking. But, for practical reasons, most players just use the fourth finger to slide to and from the note.

All root notes found here act as focal points in the given material. But not all need to be present, or present simultaneously, in music.

The
②ND String,
2ND Finger Shapes

..."The D Flat / C Sharp Shapes"

Fret

X

(Second String)

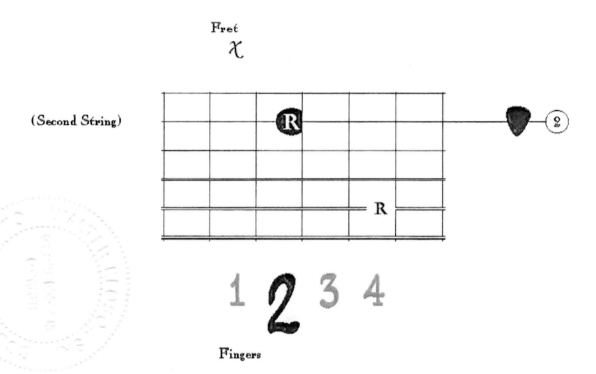

1 2 3 4

Fingers

THIS IS THE SECOND STRING SECOND FINGER SHAPE.
THE NAME COMES FROM THE LOCATION OF ITS MAIN
ROOT NOTE, WHICH IS ALONG THE SECOND STRING
AND UNDER THE SECOND FINGER HERE. THE SECOND
FINGER FRETS IT. THE OTHER ROOT NOTE THAT
REMAINS IS FOUND AN OCTAVE AWAY ON THE FIFTH
STRING. THE FOURTH FINGER REGULARLY FRETS IT.
FUNCTIONAL TENSION DICTATES THAT THE SECOND
AND FOURTH FINGERS OF THE FRETTING HAND WORK
TOGETHER WHEN PLAYING THIS MATERIAL. ⇨

Some of the guitar chord shapes associated with this MAIN ROOT NOTE ARE:

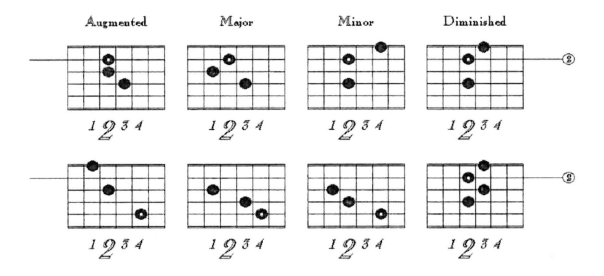

Augmented   Major   Minor   Diminished

Some of the guitar scale shapes associated with this MAIN ROOT NOTE ARE:

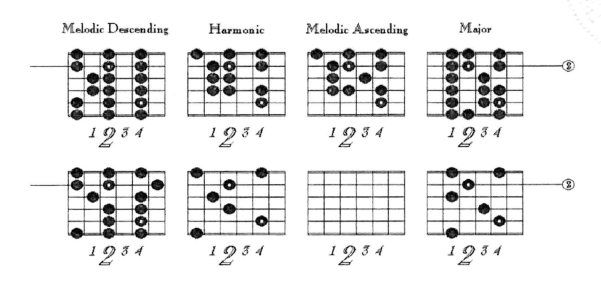

Melodic Descending   Harmonic   Melodic Ascending   Major

FURTHER COMMENTARY...

ALL SECOND STRING, SECOND FINGER SHAPES FOUND ON THE PREVIOUS PAGE FIT NEATLY INTO ANY SINGLE GUITAR POSITION. EACH SHAPE CAN ALSO BE MOVED UP AND DOWN THE NECK AT WILL, WHICH MAKES FOR SOME RICH PRACTICE MATERIAL.

THE COLLECTED SECOND STRING, SECOND FINGER MATERIAL SHOWCASES THE TECHNICAL RELATIONSHIP BETWEEN THE SECOND AND FOURTH FINGERS VERY WELL. HERE THE MATCHING OCTAVE IS TWO STRINGS AWAY AND REQUIRES NO FINGER STRETCH TO PLAY. THE TWO STRING SKIP NO FINGER STRETCH COMBO IS WHAT MAKES THIS SITUATION UNIQUE. USUALLY THE SECOND FINGER DEALS WITH A SINGLE STRING SKIP AND / OR THE FOURTH FINGER HAS TO STRETCH OR SLIDE TO THE AFFILIATED OCTAVE.

ALL ROOT NOTES, **MAIN** OR OTHERWISE, FOUND IN THE SECOND STRING SECOND FINGER SHAPES SIMPLY ACT AS LITTLE FOCAL POINTS WITHIN THE GIVEN MATERIAL. BUT NOT ALL ROOT NOTES NEED BE PRESENT, NOR PRESENT SIMULTANEOUSLY, WHEN IT COMES TO VOICING ANY GIVEN CHORD AND / OR SCALE.

THE ②ND STRING, 3RD FINGER SHAPES

..."THE D SHAPES"

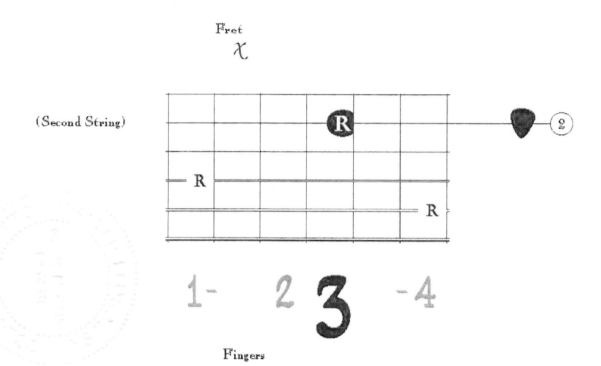

Fret
X

(Second String)

Fingers

1- 2 **3** -4

THIS IS THE SECOND STRING THIRD FINGER SHAPE.
ITS NAME COMES FROM THE **MAIN** ROOT NOTE BEING
FOUND ON THE SECOND STRING UNDER THE THIRD
FINGER. IT IS MOST NATURAL THAT THE THIRD
FINGER PLAYS IT. THE OTHER PAIR OF ROOT NOTES
ARE FOUND AN OCTAVE AWAY ON THE RESPECTIVE
FOURTH AND FIFTH STRINGS. STRETCH THE FIRST
AND FOURTH FINGER TO PLAY THOSE. NOTICE THE
THIRD AND FIRST FINGERS OF THE FRETTING HAND
HAVE THE TECHNICAL RELATIONSHIP HERE. ⇨

SOME OF THE GUITAR CHORD SHAPES ASSOCIATED WITH THIS **MAIN** ROOT NOTE ARE:

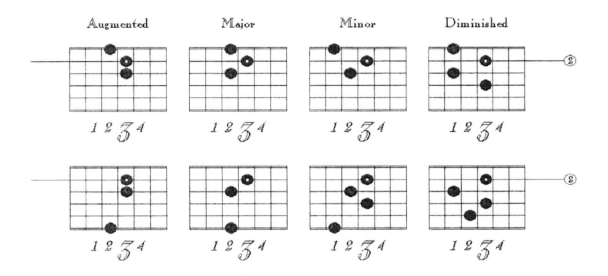

SOME OF THE GUITAR SCALE SHAPES ASSOCIATED WITH THIS **MAIN** ROOT NOTE ARE:

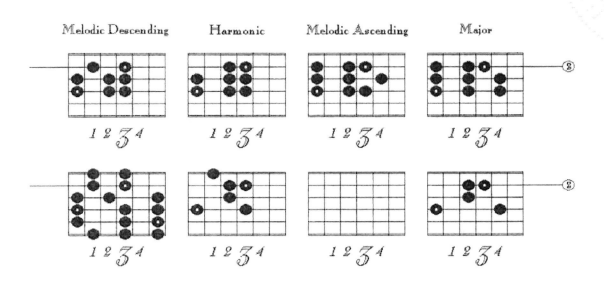

Further Commentary...

All second string third finger shapes work in any guitar position and all are movable to any other as well. Pick a position and have a go there before moving them about the neck. Compensate for fret spacing issues. In doing this, the third finger maintains a precedence in the finger work simply because the **MAIN** root note falls underneath it.

The lower pitched root note on the fourth string is the one most often paired with this particular **MAIN** root note. Once beyond the first position, the first finger must stretch to play it. The other root note found on the fifth string requires a fourth finger stretch to play, technically speaking. But,

FOR PRACTICAL REASONS, MOST JUST SLIDE INTO
IT AND FROM IT AS NEEDED.

ALL ROOT NOTES FOUND IN THESE SHAPES ACT AS
MERE FOCAL POINTS, THAT'S ALL. BUT NOT EVERY
ROOT NOTE NEEDS TO BE PRESENT, NOR PRESENT
SIMULTANEOUSLY, WHEN IT COMES TO VOICING THE
GIVEN MATERIAL.

The
②ND / ④TH String(s),
1ST & 4TH Finger Shapes

..."The E Flat / D Sharp Shapes

Fret
X

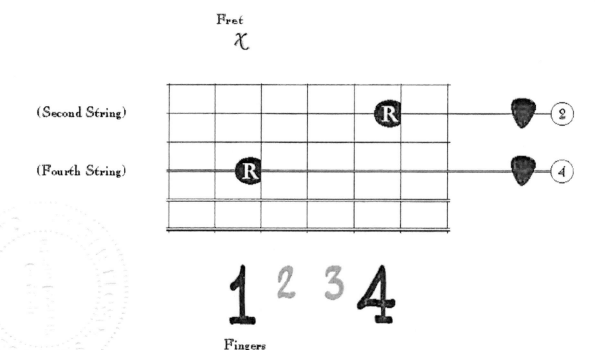

(Second String)

(Fourth String)

1 2 3 4

Fingers

THIS IS THE SECOND / FOURTH STRING(S) FIRST AND
FOURTH FINGER SHAPE, SO NAMED FROM THE **MAIN
ROOT NOTE(S)** AS FOUND ON THE SECOND / FOURTH
STRING(S) UNDER THE FIRST AND FOURTH FINGERS
OF THE FRETTING HAND. HERE, THE FIRST AND / OR
FOURTH FINGERS PLAY ONE OR BOTH OF THE **MAIN
ROOT NOTE(S)**, NOT THE USUAL SECOND OR THE
THIRD FINGERS. FUNCTIONAL TENSION DICTATES
THAT THE FIRST AND FOURTH FINGERS BE INVOLVED
WHEN PLAYING THIS MATERIAL. ⇨

SOME OF THE GUITAR CHORD SHAPES ASSOCIATED WITH THIS MAIN ROOT NOTE(S) ARE:

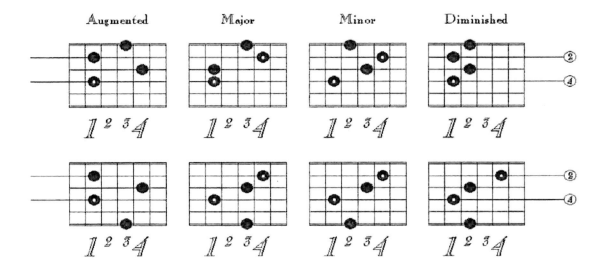

SOME OF THE GUITAR SCALE SHAPES ASSOCIATED WITH THIS MAIN ROOT NOTE(S) ARE:

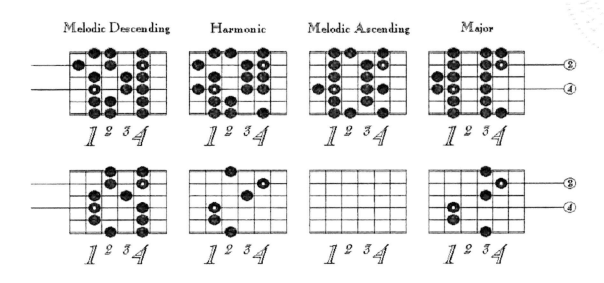

FURTHER COMMENTARY...

ALL SECOND / FOURTH STRING(S) FIRST AND FOURTH FINGER SHAPES, AS FOUND ON THE PREVIOUS PAGE, FIT THE FRETTING HAND NICELY AND WORK IN ANY SINGLE POSITION ON THE GUITAR. AND ALL OF THESE SHAPES CAN BE MOVED UP AND DOWN THE NECK TO ANY OTHER POSITION AS WELL.

NOTICE THAT HERE THERE ARE TWO **MAIN** ROOT NOTES PRESENT IN THIS SHAPE, AND NOT ONE, PLUS NO ADDITIONAL OCTAVES. CONSEQUENTLY, THE FIRST AND FOURTH FINGERS OF THE FRETTING HAND MAY PLAY THE **MAIN** ROOT NOTES INDIVIDUALLY, LIKE IN AN ARPEGGIO OR SCALE, OR IT MAY CHOOSE TO VOICE THEM SIMULTANEOUSLY, LIKE IN A CHORD. BUT NO MATTER THE CHOICE, IT IS THE FIRST AND FOURTH FINGERS ON THE FRETTING HAND THAT MAINTAIN A

DISTINCT PRECEDENCE IN THE FINGER WORK AS BOTH MAIN ROOT NOTE(S) FALL UNDERNEATH THEM.

ALL ROOT NOTES FOUND IN THE SECOND / FOURTH STRING(S) FIRST AND FOURTH FINGER SHAPES ACT AS MUSICAL FOCAL POINTS WITHIN THE GIVEN MATERIAL. BUT KEEP IN MIND, BOTH MAIN ROOT NOTE(S) NEED NOT BE PRESENT, NOR PRESENT SIMULTANEOUSLY, WHEN IT COMES TO PLAYING THE GIVEN MATERIAL.

THE ④TH STRING, 2ND FINGER SHAPES

..."THE E SHAPES"

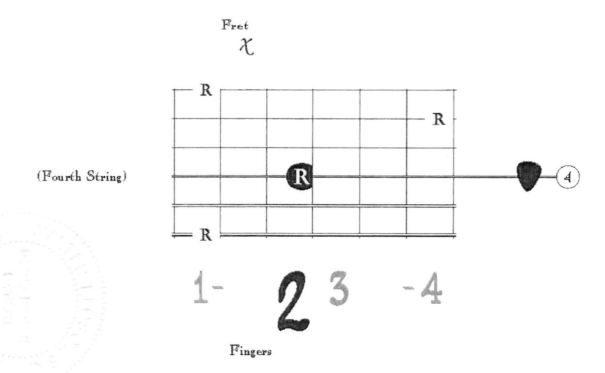

Fret

X

R

R

(Fourth String)   R   4

R

R

1- **2** 3 -4

Fingers

THIS IS THE FOURTH STRING SECOND FINGER SHAPE.
ITS MAIN ROOT NOTE IS LOCATED ON THE FOURTH
STRING UNDER THE SECOND FINGER, AND IT IS
MOST NATURAL FOR THE SECOND FINGER TO PLAY
IT. THE OTHER ROOT NOTES THAT REMAIN ARE
FOUND ON THE RESPECTIVE FIRST, SECOND AND
SIXTH STRINGS. STRETCH THE FIRST FINGER, AND
STRETCH FOURTH FINGER, TO PLAY THOSE. THE
SECOND AND FOURTH FINGERS OF THE FRETTING
HAND HAVE THE WORKING RELATIONSHIP HERE. ⇨

SOME OF THE GUITAR CHORD SHAPES ASSOCIATED WITH THIS **MAIN** ROOT NOTE ARE:

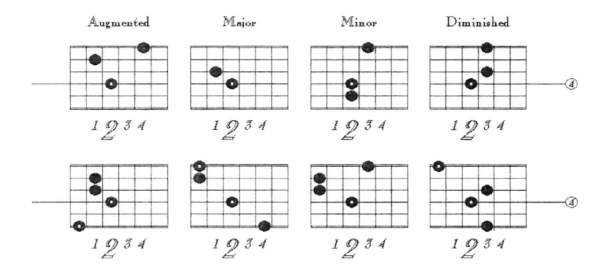

SOME OF THE GUITAR SCALE SHAPES ASSOCIATED WITH THIS **MAIN** ROOT NOTE ARE:

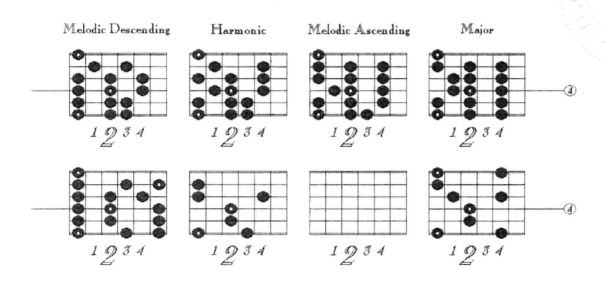

FURTHER COMMENTARY...

ALL FOURTH STRING SECOND FINGER SHAPES WORK WELL IN ANY SINGLE POSITION ON THE GUITAR AND ALL ARE MOVABLE TO ANY OTHER POSITION AS WELL. WHEN VOICING THEM, THE SECOND FINGER ON THE FRETTING HAND MAINTAINS A DISTINCT PRECEDENCE IN THE FINGERING AS THE **MAIN** ROOT NOTE FALLS UNDERNEATH IT.

THE LOWER OCTAVE ROOT NOTE, FOUND ON THE SIXTH STRING, AND THE HIGHER OCTAVE ROOT NOTE, FOUND ON THE FIRST STRING, ARE OFTEN PAIRED WITH THIS **MAIN** ROOT NOTE. AND NO MATTER WHICH IS USED, A STRETCHED FIRST FINGER WILL BE INVOLVED AT SOME POINT. THE OTHER ROOT NOTE THAT REMAINS IS FOUND ON THE SECOND STRING. IT IS THE SAME PITCH AS, OR IN

UNISON WITH, THE ROOT NOTE ON THE ADJACENT FIRST STRING. IT REQUIRES A FOURTH FINGER STRETCH TO PLAY, TECHNICALLY SPEAKING. BUT MOST PLAYERS JUST SLIDE INTO IT AND FROM IT WITH THE FOURTH FINGER AS NEEDED.

THERE ARE SEVERAL ROOT NOTES PRESENT IN THE FOURTH STRING SECOND FINGER SHAPE, AND ALL ROOT NOTES FOUND HERE ACT AS MUSICAL FOCAL POINTS WITHIN THE GIVEN MATERIAL TO BE SURE. BUT NOT EACH AND EVERY ROOT NOTE NEEDS TO BE PRESENT, OR PRESENT SIMULTANEOUSLY, IN ANY CHORD OR SCALE VOICING.

The
④TH STRING,
3RD FINGER SHAPES

..."THE F SHAPES"

Fret

X

R

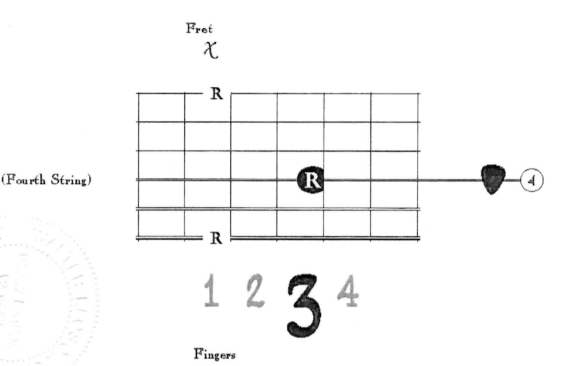

(Fourth String)

R   4

R

1 2 **3** 4

Fingers

This is the fourth string third finger shape. It's named after the **MAIN** root note as found on the fourth string under the third finger. The third finger plays this **MAIN** root note. The octave root notes found on the first and sixth strings are often paired with it as well. Use the first finger to play either of those. Functional tension dictates that the third and first fingers of the fretting hand work in consort here. ⇨

SOME OF THE GUITAR CHORD SHAPES ASSOCIATED WITH THIS <u>MAIN</u> ROOT NOTE ARE:

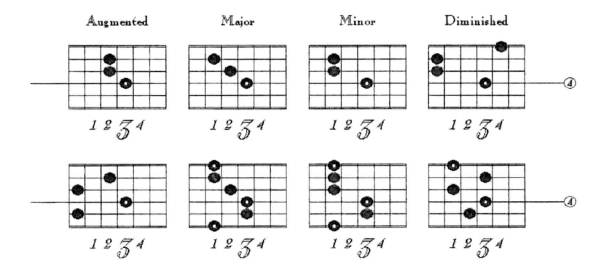

SOME OF THE GUITAR SCALE SHAPES ASSOCIATED WITH THIS <u>MAIN</u> ROOT NOTE ARE:

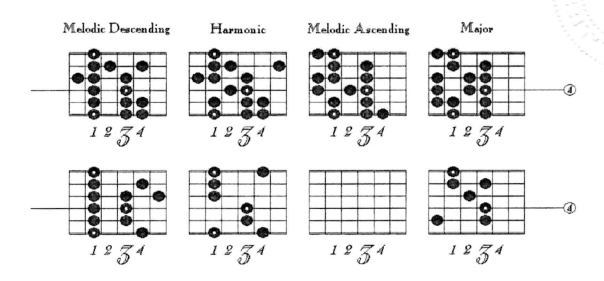

Further Commentary...

All of the fourth string third finger shapes that are found on the previous page work in any single position on the guitar and all are movable to any other position as well. It is best to work them out in one position before moving them about the neck.

When voicing these chords and scales the third finger on the fretting hand maintains a distinct precedence in the fingering simply because the **main** root note falls underneath it. It is quite natural.

When including the sixth string and / or the higher octave root note found on the first string, do not stretch the first finger.

All of the root notes found in the fourth string third finger shape material act as focal points to use for practice or for any other musical purpose. But understand that not every root note need be present, nor present simultaneously, when voicing any given chord or scale.

THE
TWELVE SHAPES
APPENDIX

Fret

𝑥

(First String)

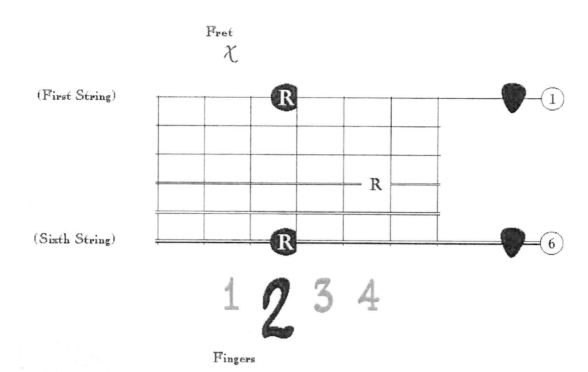

R

R

R

(Sixth String)

1

6

1 **2** 3 4

Fingers

The
①ˢᵗ / ⑥ᵗʰ String(s),
2ⁿᵈ Finger Shapes

..."The G Flat / F Sharp Shapes"

①ˢᵀ ⑥ᵀᴴ, 2ᴺᴰ – CHORDS

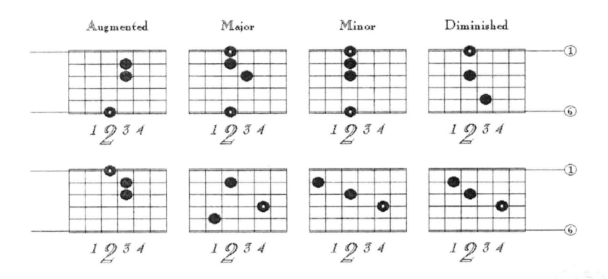

Augmented   Major   Minor   Diminished

①ˢᵀ ⑥ᵀᴴ, 2ᴺᴰ – SCALES

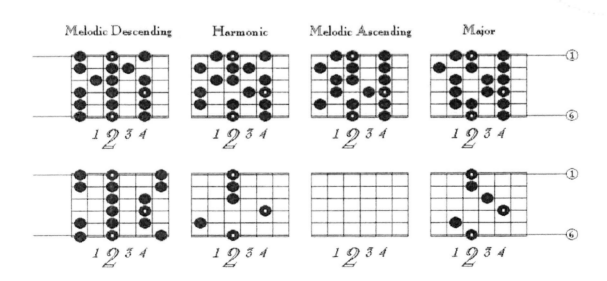

Melodic Descending   Harmonic   Melodic Ascending   Major

Fret

𝒳

(First String)

(Sixth String)

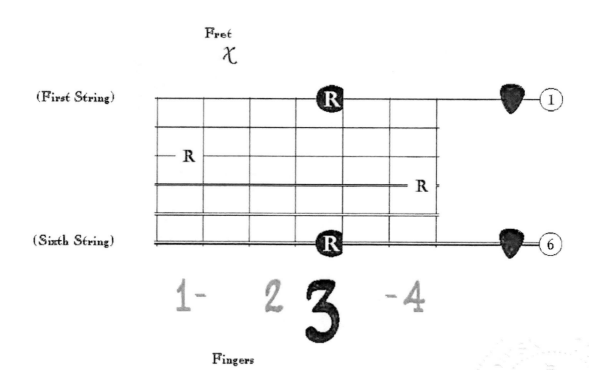

1 -   2 **3** - 4

Fingers

THE
①ˢᵗ / ⑥ᵀᴴ STRING(S),
3ᴿᴰ FINGER SHAPES

...·"THE G SHAPES"

①ˢᵀ ⑥ᵀᴴ, 3ᴿᴰ - Chords

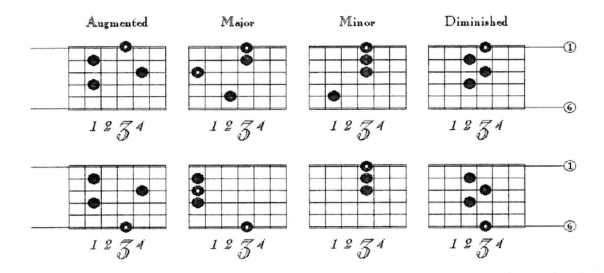

①ˢᵀ ⑥ᵀᴴ, 3ᴿᴰ - Scales

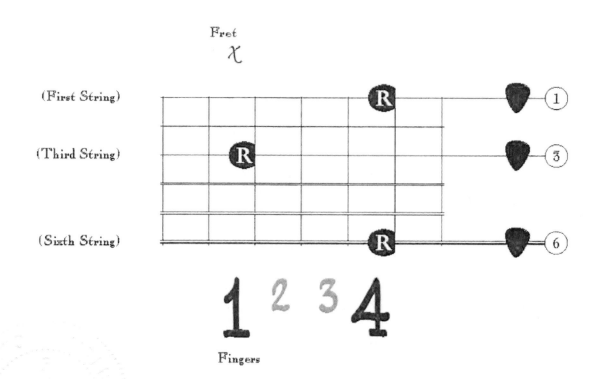

THE
①ST / ③RD / ⑥TH STRING(S),
1ST & 4TH FINGER SHAPES

..."THE A FLAT / G SHARP SHAPES"

①ˢᵀ ③ᴿᴰ ⑥ᵀᴴ, 1ˢᵀ 4ᵀᴴ — CHORDS

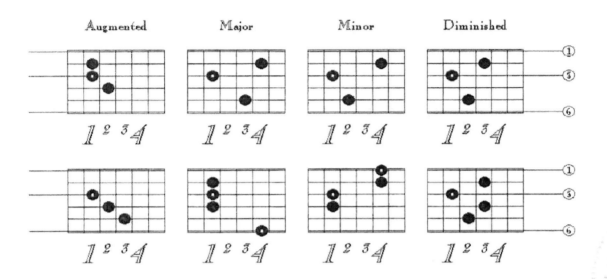

①ˢᵀ ③ᴿᴰ ⑥ᵀᴴ, 1ˢᵀ 4ᵀᴴ — SCALES

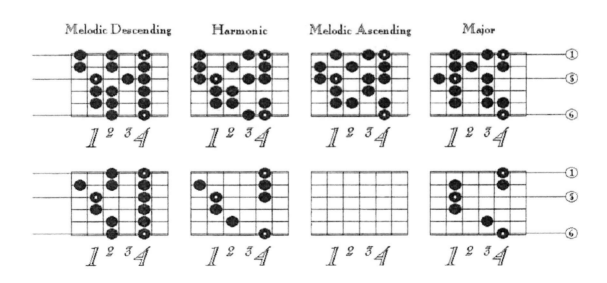

Fret

X

(Third String)

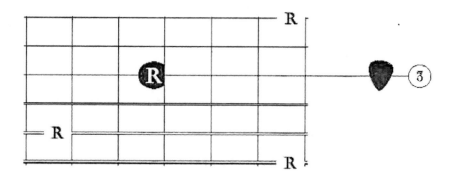

R

③

1- **2** 3 -4

Fingers

THE
③RD STRING,
2ND FINGER SHAPES

..."THE A SHAPES"

③RD, 2ND - CHORDS

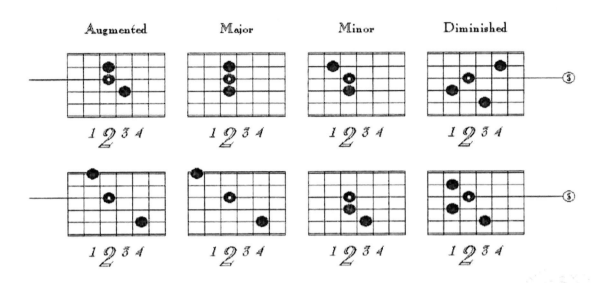

③RD, 2ND - SCALES

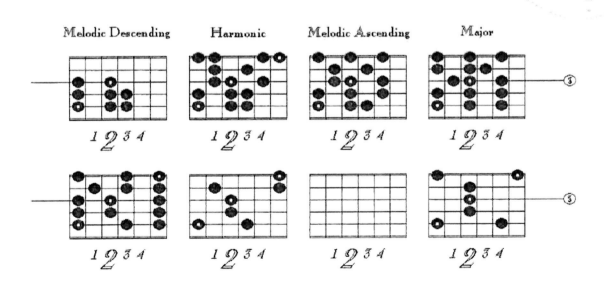

Fret
X

(Third String)

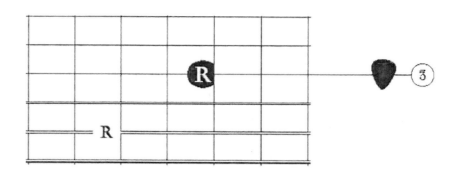

③

1 2 **3** 4

Fingers

THE
③ᴿᴰ STRING,
3ᴿᴰ FINGER SHAPES

...*"THE B FLAT / A SHARP SHAPES"*

③ᴿᴰ, 3ᴿᴰ — CHORDS

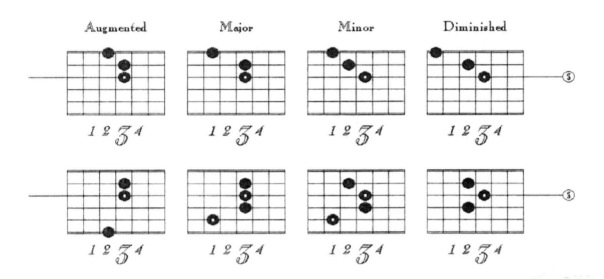

③ᴿᴰ, 3ᴿᴰ — SCALES

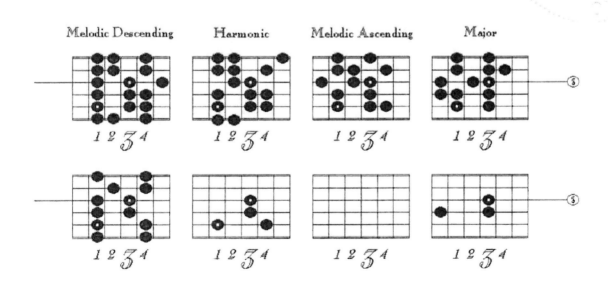

Fret

χ

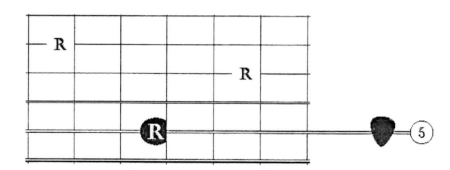

(Fifth String)

R

R

R

⑤

1- **2** 3 4

Fingers

THE
⑤TH STRING,
2ND FINGER SHAPES

..."THE 8 SHAPES"

⑤TH, 2ND – CHORDS

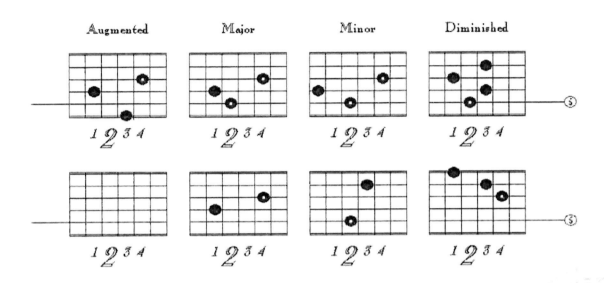

Augmented	Major	Minor	Diminished
1 2 3 4	1 2 3 4	1 2 3 4	1 2 3 4

1 2 3 4	1 2 3 4	1 2 3 4	1 2 3 4

⑤TH, 2ND – SCALES

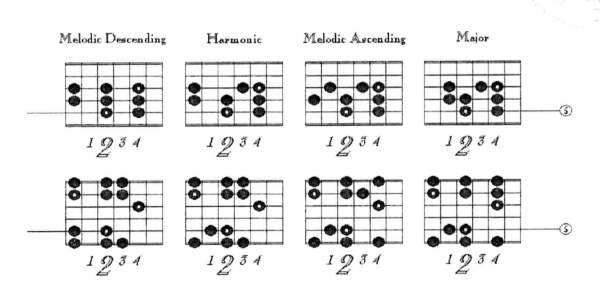

Melodic Descending	Harmonic	Melodic Ascending	Major
1 2 3 4	1 2 3 4	1 2 3 4	1 2 3 4

1 2 3 4	1 2 3 4	1 2 3 4	1 2 3 4

Fret

χ

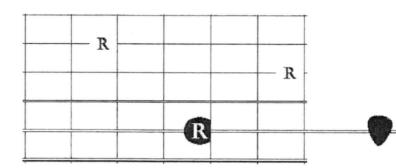

(Fifth String)

1 2 **3** -4

Fingers

THE
⑤TH STRING,
3RD FINGER SHAPES

...."THE C SHAPES"

⑤ᵀᴴ, 3ᴿᴰ – CHORDS

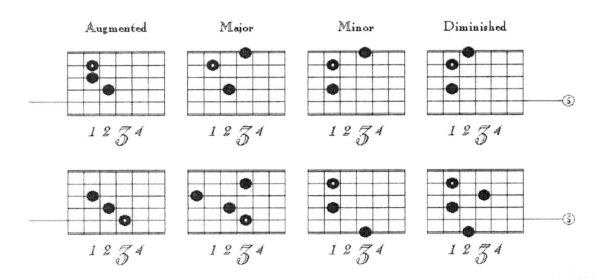

Augmented   Major   Minor   Diminished

1 2 3 4   1 2 3 4   1 2 3 4   1 2 3 4

1 2 3 4   1 2 3 4   1 2 3 4   1 2 3 4

⑤ᵀᴴ, 3ᴿᴰ – SCALES

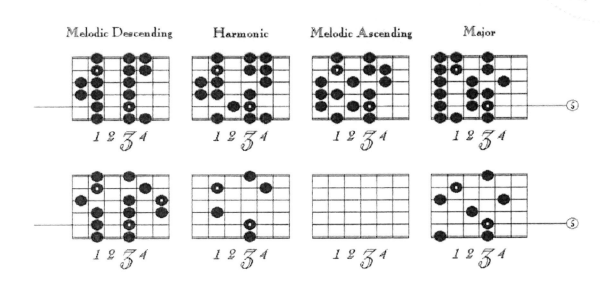

Melodic Descending   Harmonic   Melodic Ascending   Major

1 2 3 4   1 2 3 4   1 2 3 4   1 2 3 4

1 2 3 4   1 2 3 4   1 2 3 4   1 2 3 4

Fret

X

(Second String)

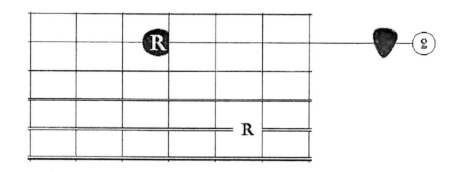

②

1 **2** 3 4

Fingers

The
②ND String,
2ND Finger Shapes

..."The D Flat / C Sharp Shapes"

②ND, 2ND - CHORDS

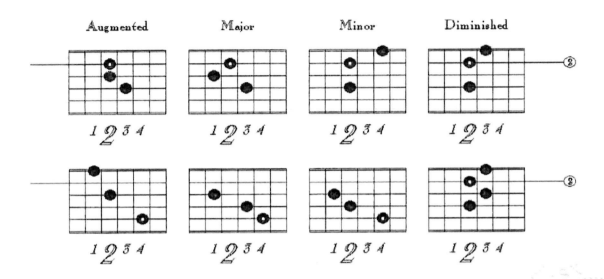

Augmented   Major   Minor   Diminished

1 2 3 4   1 2 3 4   1 2 3 4   1 2 3 4

1 2 3 4   1 2 3 4   1 2 3 4   1 2 3 4

②ND, 2ND - SCALES

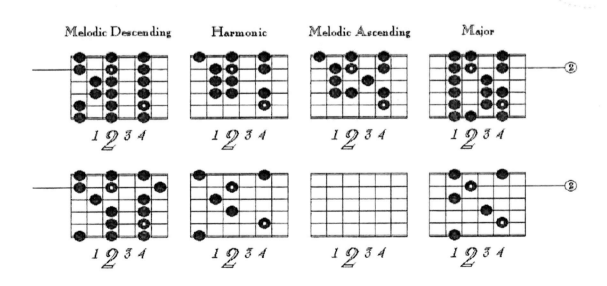

Melodic Descending   Harmonic   Melodic Ascending   Major

1 2 3 4   1 2 3 4   1 2 3 4   1 2 3 4

1 2 3 4   1 2 3 4   1 2 3 4   1 2 3 4

Fret
χ

(Second String)

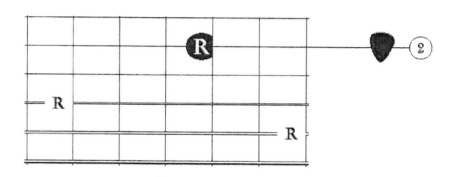

1- 2 **3** -4

Fingers

The
②ND String,
3RD Finger Shapes

..."The D Shapes"

②ND, 3RD – CHORDS

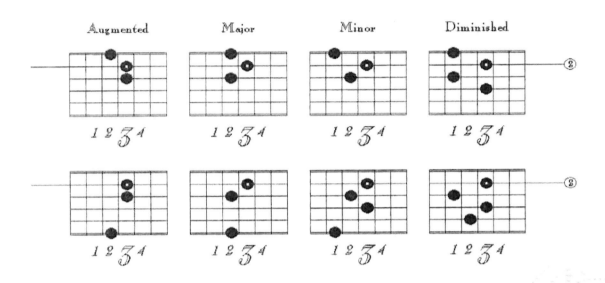

Augmented   Major   Minor   Diminished

1 2 3 4   1 2 3 4   1 2 3 4   1 2 3 4

1 2 3 4   1 2 3 4   1 2 3 4   1 2 3 4

②ND, 3RD – SCALES

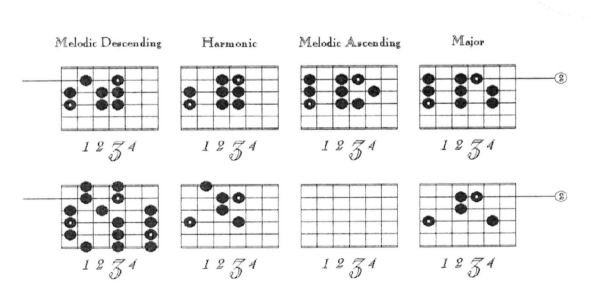

Melodic Descending   Harmonic   Melodic Ascending   Major

1 2 3 4   1 2 3 4   1 2 3 4   1 2 3 4

1 2 3 4   1 2 3 4   1 2 3 4   1 2 3 4

Fret

χ

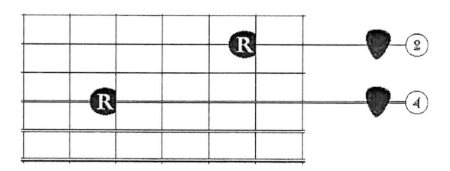

(Second String)

(Fourth String)

1 ² ³ 4

Fingers

THE
②ND / ④TH STRING(S),
1ST & 4TH FINGER SHAPES

..."THE E FLAT / D SHARP SHAPES

②ND ④TH, 1ST 4TH - CHORDS

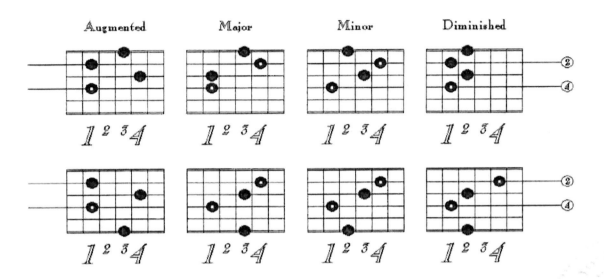

②ND ④TH, 1ST 4TH - SCALES

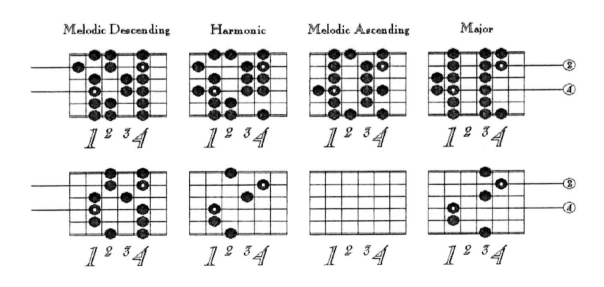

Fret

χ

R

R

(Fourth String)

R

R

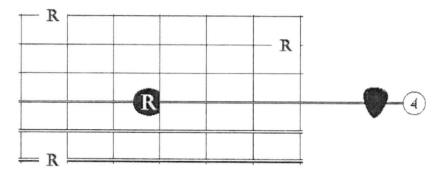

④

1- **2** 3 -4

Fingers

THE
④TH STRING,
2ND FINGER SHAPES

...."THE E SHAPES"

④TH, 2ND - CHORDS

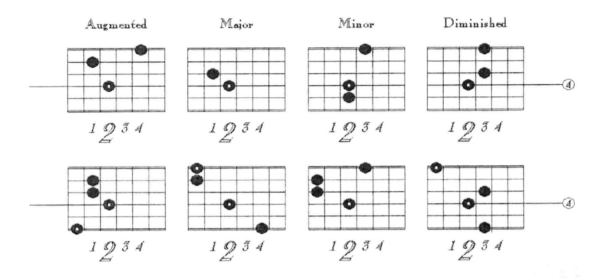

Augmented   Major   Minor   Diminished

1 2 3 4   1 2 3 4   1 2 3 4   1 2 3 4

④

1 2 3 4   1 2 3 4   1 2 3 4   1 2 3 4

④

④TH, 2ND - SCALES

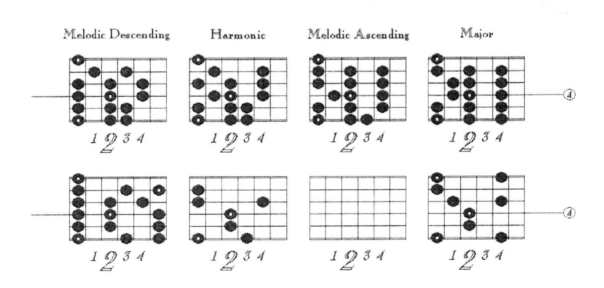

Melodic Descending   Harmonic   Melodic Ascending   Major

1 2 3 4   1 2 3 4   1 2 3 4   1 2 3 4

④

1 2 3 4   1 2 3 4   1 2 3 4   1 2 3 4

④

Fret
χ

R

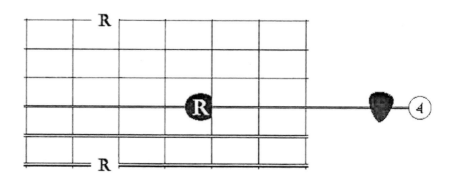

(Fourth String)

R   ④

R

1 2 **3** 4

Fingers

The
④TH String,
3RD Finger Shapes

..."The F Shapes"

④TH, 3RD - CHORDS

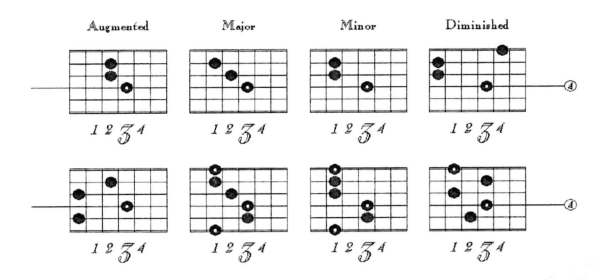

Augmented   Major   Minor   Diminished

1 2 3 4   1 2 3 4   1 2 3 4   1 2 3 4

1 2 3 4   1 2 3 4   1 2 3 4   1 2 3 4

④TH, 3RD - SCALES

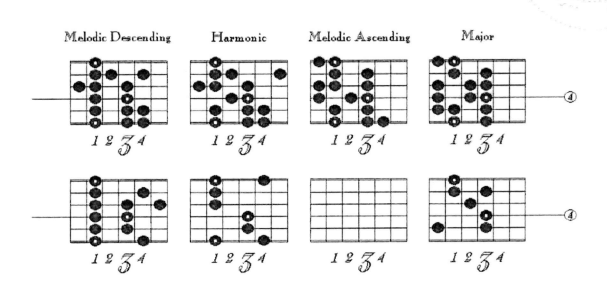

Melodic Descending   Harmonic   Melodic Ascending   Major

1 2 3 4   1 2 3 4   1 2 3 4   1 2 3 4

1 2 3 4   1 2 3 4   1 2 3 4   1 2 3 4

CPSIA information can be obtained at www.ICGtesting.com
Printed in the USA
LVOW09s2202020316

477486LV00024B/667/P